STALIN

The dictator of the Union of Soviet Socialist Republics

THE HISTORY HOUR

CONTENTS

FROM GEORGIA
WITH RAGE

❦

Ideas are more powerful than guns. We would not let our enemies have guns, why should we let them have ideas.

Joseph Stalin

❦

Joseph Stalin.

❦

He is one of the most infamous figures of the 20th Century, lionized by his followers and excoriated by the rest of the world. His name has become synonymous with mass murder and political oppression. His history is bloody, his story is complex, and his influence continues to this day.

঵঺঻

Everyone thinks they know him, but who was Stalin, really?

UNLOVED CHILD

❧❦❧

The future Stalin was born Iosef Djugashvili in the tiny Georgian town of Gori in December 1879. The exact date of his birth is obscure, partially because of the difference between the Russian and Western calendars, and partially because he himself altered certain biographical details later in his life. He was the only surviving son of Vissarion "Beso" Djugashvili, an unsuccessful cobbler, and Yekaterina "Keke" Geladze, who was a pious woman who worked as a laundress and seamstress for wealthier families. There is some question whether Beso was truly Stalin's father, and Stalin himself certainly would have been in no hurry to claim him if he was. The future Soviet leader said that his real father was a priest, who remained unnamed.

❧❦❧

BESO WAS A VIOLENT MAN, a raging alcoholic and an abusive husband and father. He beat Iosef repeatedly and often beat

3

Keke in Iosef's presence. Ultimately Keke took Iosef and left Beso behind, moving in with a family friend, Russian Orthodox priest Father Christopher Charkviani. At the age of 7, he contracted smallpox, a disease which nearly killed him and left his face pockmarked for the rest of his life.

❧

KEKE WAS a pious woman who desperately wanted her only son to be a member of the clergy, and her ambitions for Iosef were encouraged by his intellect and by Charkviani's support. In 1888, at the age of 10, he was admitted into the Gori Church School, a privilege that was normally reserved for the children of clergy. Considering his later assertion, it might be that Charkviani was his true father, but that is only supposition.

❧

HE EXCELLED IN ACADEMICS, with special ability in drama, painting and poetry. He was a talented student, but he often got into fights. At 12, he was struck by a horse-drawn buggy, which resulted in a terrible injury to his left arm. The arm never fully healed and was permanently shortened and bent.

❧

IN AUGUST 1894, he was enrolled in the Spiritual Seminary in Tiflis, one of 600 young aspirants to the priesthood. A religious life was his mother's dream, not his own, and he began to rebel. He was frequently disciplined for lack of respect for his seniors and for announcing that he was an atheist. Stalin continued to excel academically, showing a great gift for memorizing Bible passages, and he began to write poetry under the name of Soselo. His poems, which were very patriotic and nationalist in tone, were published in the newspaper *Iveria* and became quite popular.

಄಄

HIS INTEREST in school completely waned, and to satisfy his curious mind, he began to attend a forbidden book club, reading works like *Das Kapital* by Karl Marx and *The Patricide* by Alexander Kazbegi. It was from the latter work that he took a nickname, "Koba", based on the ruffian hero of the work. Given his own history, one can certainly suppose that the title alone held his interest.

಄಄

STALIN BECAME ENAMORED of Marxism and socialism, no doubt inspired by the hardships his own family had endured on the lowest rung of the social ladder. It was during this period when he began to attend secret workers' meetings, where he met Silibistro "Silva" Jibladze, the socialist who had founded *Mesame Dasi* ("Third Group"), a Georgian revolutionary unit.

಄಄

DISSATISFIED with his studies and wholly embracing Marxism, Iosef Djugashvili dropped out of the Seminary in 1899.

REVOLUTIONARY ROOTS

☙❧

I n October 1899, Stalin took work as a meteorologist at an observatory in Tiflis. On the side, he began giving classes in socialist theory, and like Aristotle, he began to gather followers to his radical and persuasive message.

☙❧

WHEN MAY DAY 1900 rolled around, Stalin co-organized a secret mass meeting of workers, where he successfully urged the men to strike. This brought him to the attention of the Okhrana, the Tsar's secret police, who tried to arrest him in March 1901. He escaped their net and went into hiding, living with friends and supporters and sleeping on couches, a habit he would retain until the end of his life.

☙❧

WHILE STILL IN HIDING, he organized a massive workers'

demonstration that took place on May Day 1900. Over three thousand workers clashed with authorities. There were no fatalities, but the resulting unrest presaged things to come.

※

IN NOVEMBER OF 1901, Stalin was elected to the Tiflis Committee of the Russian Social Democratic Labor Party (RSDLP), which was a Marxist political faction that had been founded in 1898. That same month, he relocated to Batumi, where he let fly with such violent rhetoric and ideas that the local socialists began to believe that he might be an *agent provocateur* working for the Tsar. Nothing could have been farther from the truth.

※

HE TOOK work at a Rothschild refinery storehouse, and he wasted no time in organizing the workers and convincing them to go on strike two times. Several of the strike leaders were arrested, so he decided to organize a demonstration in protest. The demonstration grew out of control, with protestors storming the prison. The authorities shot into the crowd, and 13 striking workers were killed. In anger, he organized a demonstration at the mass funeral for these 13 men. This time, there were no fatalities.

PRISON

❧

The Okhrana finally caught up with Stalin in April 1902, when he was arrested and sent to Batumi Prison. In short order, he was moved to a more secure prison, Kutaisi. He made himself a nuisance with his rough behavior, and in 1903, he was exiled to Siberia for the first time, being sentenced to three years of internal exile and sent to the town of Novaya Uda.

❧

WHILE STALIN WAS AWAY, the RSDLP split into two factions: the Bolsheviks, led by Vladimir Lenin, and the Mensheviks, who were led by Julius Martov. For Stalin, who hated many of the men on the Menshevik side, it was an easy choice to align himself with the Bolsheviks.

❧

IN THE MEANTIME, he had to get out of prison. He made two escape attempts. The first was defeated by a case of frostbite that forced him to turn back, but the second succeeded, and he returned to Tiflis. Once he was there, he began to co-edit the newspaper *Proletariatis Brdzola* ("Proletarian Struggle") with Philip Makharadze. He attracted the ire of members of the RSDLP by calling for Georgian Marxists to be split from the Russian party, for which he was accused of being contrary to the international hopes of the Marxists, and he narrowly escaped being expelled from the party.

❧ II ❧

WINDS OF CHANGE
BEGIN TO BLOW

๑๛

The people who cast the votes don't decide an election, the people who count the votes do.

Joseph Stalin

๑๛

In 1905, during a demonstration in St. Petersburg, Tsarist government troops massacred between 200 and 1000 striking workers (the number is not clear) who marched on the Winter Palace to present Tsar Nicholas II with a petition and demands. Unrest swept through the Russian Empire all the way to Georgia, where ethnic tensions erupted between the Armenians and the Azeri. Stalin was in Baku when the Armenians and Azeri conducted their hate-filled killing sprees, leaving 2000 dead in their wake. Stalin blamed the Tsar for the deaths, claiming publicly that Nicholas II had instigated ethnic unrest with pogroms against the Jewish and Armenian citizens of the Empire in order to prop up his ever-more insecure rule.

A WARRIOR FOR THE FIRST TIME

❦

During the Armenian/Azeri conflict, Stalin formed Bolshevik Battle Squads with the stated aim of keeping the two sides separated. Meanwhile, he used the unrest and the Battle Squads as cover so that he could steal some expensive printing equipment.

❦

As violence spread through Georgia, both the Bolsheviks and the Mensheviks formed more and more Battle Squads. Occasionally the two groups coordinated their efforts, like when they attacked both government Cossack troops and the pro-Tsar Back Hundreds, an ultra-nationalist group. Most of the time, the Bolshevik Battle Squads occupied themselves with disarming local police and troops, stealing from government arsenals and running detailed protection rackets on local businesses and mining outfits.

❧❧❧

THE 1905 REVOLUTION ended when Tsar Nicholas II signed the new Constitution of 1906, which created the multiparty state house called the Duma, and which reduced his own role from absolute ruler to a constitutional monarchy. The first true war in Stalin's life was over.

BACK TO POLITICS

❧

In November 1905, Stalin was elected as the Georgian Bolsheviks' representative at an upcoming Bolshevik conference that was to take place in St. Petersburg. When he arrived, he was met by Nadezhda Krupskaya, who told him that the meeting had been moved to the Grand Duchy of Finland, and that her husband wished to meet him. Her husband was Vladimir Lenin.

❧

THE TWO MEN met for the first time in Finland, and Stalin greatly respected Lenin, and Lenin, for his part, recognized the powerful force of personality that his Georgian contemporary possessed. They soon formed a formidable partnership.

❧

LENIN WANTED a Bolshevik candidate to run for one of the seats in the newly-created Duma, but Stalin thought that the concept of working for change from the inside was a waste of time and effort.

❧

NEVERTHELESS, Stalin remained faithful to the RSDLP and attended the fourth Party Conference in Stockholm in April 1906. There the Mensheviks, who controlled the party, criticized his Bolsheviks for using robbery to enrich the party. Stalin, who organized many of these robberies with his group, the Outfit, ignored them, but he took note of the Mensheviks by name.

❧

IN JULY 1906, he married Ketevan "Kato" Svanidze, and in March 1907, Stalin's first child, a son named Yakov, was born. He did not let his new domestic status distract him from the Party for very long.

❧

FROM MAY THROUGH JUNE 1907, he attended the fifth RSDLP Conference, which was held in London. Again, the Mensheviks warned against the use of violence, and again the Bolsheviks, with Lenin and Stalin at the helm, ignored their warnings. While at the conference, the Bolsheviks elected their own ruling body, which they called the Bolshevik Center. On the way back from London, in Berlin, Lenin and Stalin met with other members of the Bolshevik wing of the Party. Among those attending were Lenin, Stalin, Leonid Krasin, Alexander Bogdonov and Maxim Litvinov. Stalin, who was increasingly well-known in criminal circles as Koba (the name he'd taken from *The Patricide*), was made responsible for "appropriations" along with Stalin's childhood friend and Marxist convert, the Armenian Simon Ter-Petrossian ("Kamo"). The Centre decided that Koba and Kamo, should rob the Imperial Bank in Tiflis.

❧

ON THE DAY of the robbery, June 26, 1907, the authorities had heard that some sort of action was being prepared by the underground, and an increased presence of guards and troops had assembled in Yerevan Square, near the bank and the Seminary. When the coach carrying money intended for the bank appeared in the square, the Bolsheviks, led by Kamo in a cavalry officer's uniform, attacked with revolvers and home-made bombs. When the smoke cleared, forty people were dead and the Bolsheviks had made away with some 19,000 rubles. None of the Bolsheviks were arrested at that time, although Kamo was later arrested in Austria while trying to pass marked 500-ruble notes. He was initially sentenced to death for his activities (which included cutting a man's heart out of his chest) but his sentence was commuted to life in prison due to insanity. He was released from prison after the 1917 Revolution.

❧

LENIN and his wife fled to Finland and thence to Switzerland. Stalin went back into hiding in Georgia, and the other organizers escaped police. Kamo was the only one of the Bolsheviks who ever stood trial.

❧

STALIN'S ROLE in the robbery seems to have been in an organizational and supervisory capacity, but in later years the story of his involvement has been somewhat exaggerated.

☙❧

IN LATER YEARS, Kamo was made an official in Soviet Customs, until he was struck by a car and killed in 1922. Some have speculated that his death was ordered by Stalin.

MORE POLITICS, MORE PRISON

꧁❀꧂

S talin, Kato and Yakov moved to Baku. There he was confronted by Mensheviks in the RSDLP regarding the robbery and other criminal offenses that he and the Outfit had been carrying out, including kidnap-for-ransom and a protection racket. As he had done at the party conferences, Stalin ignored them, but noted their names. In short order, the Bolsheviks took control of the Georgian branch of the RSDLP, and criticism of his methods stopped.

꧁❀꧂

STALIN BECAME the editor of the Bolshevik newspapers *Bakinsky Proletary* and *Gudok ("Whistle")* and attended the Seventh Congress of the Second International in Stuttgart in August 1907. His personal life took a downturn when Kato died of typhus in November 1907. At her funeral, he told a friend, "This creature softened my heart of stone. She died and with her died my last warm feelings for people." He left their son with his late wife's family in Tiflis and returned to Baku, where he and the Outfit continued to extort, kidnap, rob and counterfeit.

☙❧

HIS POSITION among the Bolsheviks was gaining power, and in early 1908, he went to Geneva to meet with Lenin and a prominent Russian Marxist named Georgi Plekhanov. He took a dislike to Plekhanov, but his admiration for Lenin remained unchanged.

☙❧

THE OKHRANA CAUGHT up with him in March 1908, and he was again arrested and sent to Bailov Prison with other Bolsheviks. He led his fellow party members in discussion groups, and from prison, he ordered the killing of people he suspected were informants for the authorities. He was sentenced to two years of exile in Siberia and was sent to Solvychegodsk in Vologda Province in February 1909. By June 1909, he had escaped from prison, disguising himself as a woman and fleeing to Kotlas, then to St. Petersburg. He was again arrested in 1910 and sent back to Solvychegodsk.

☙❧

IN SIBERIA, he indulged in love affairs with several women, including his landlady, Maria Kuzakova, who gave birth to his son Konstantin in 1911. Stalin never open acknowledged Konstantin, who was later compelled to sign an agreement to remain silent about his parentage.

꧁꧂

WHEN HIS EXILE OFFICIALLY ENDED, Stalin was given permission to move to Vologda, where he stayed for two months. During this time, he had another affair, this time with seventeen-year-old Pelageya Onufrieva. He returned to St. Petersburg, where he was again arrested in September 1911 and returned to Vologda for another three-year sentence of internal exile.

꧁꧂

WHILE HE WAS IN PRISON, the first Bolshevik Central Committee was elected at the party conference in Prague. Afterward, Lenin and Grigori Zinoviev personally invited Stalin to join the Central Committee. It was a position he would hold for the rest of his life.

꧁꧂

HE ESCAPED from his exile once again and returned to St. Petersburg in February 1912. Lenin, who had hopes that Stalin could bring ethnic minorities to the party based upon his Georgian background, ordered him to turn a Bolshevik weekly newspaper, *Zvezda* ("Star") into a daily paper called *Pravda* ("Truth"). The new daily was launched in April 1912, and Stalin's position as editor was kept secret.

꧁꧂

IT WAS at this point that Iosef Djugashvili, a/k/a Soselo, a/k/a Koba, took the name Stalin, meaning "Man of steel".

꧁꧂

IN MAY 1912, he was arrested for yet another time. He was sent to Shpatertry Prison, and from there back to Siberia to serve a sentence of exile for three years. He arrived in Narym, Siberia, in July 1912 and took a room with fellow Bolshevik Yakov Sverdlov. After two months, Stalin and Sverdlov escaped and returned to St. Petersburg, where Stalin continued to edit *Pravda*.

⚜

IN OCTOBER 1912, six Bolsheviks and six Mensheviks were elected to the Duma. Stalin wrote articles in *Pravda* calling for the two sides of the party to reconcile, something that was sharply criticized by Lenin. Lenin felt so strongly about the subject that he twice met with Stalin in person in the city of Krakow. Stalin withdrew his support for reconciliation after these meetings.

⚜

STALIN TRAVELED to Vienna in January 1913 to discuss "the national question" – the problem of how to bring Russia's many ethnic minorities to the Party. He published *Marxism and the National Question* under the name K. Stalin. The article impressed Lenin and secured his reputation with the Bolsheviks.

⚜

HE WAS AGAIN ARRESTED in February 1913, sentenced to four years in exile in Siberia, and sent to Turukhansk. The authorities continued to relocate him, sending him ever closer to the Arctic Circle to places more distant and more difficult to escape. After several moves, he ended up in Kureika in March 1914. While he was there, he had another affair, this time with 13-year-old Lidia Pereprygia. She gave birth to a child in December 1914, but the baby soon died. Lidia would give Stalin another son, Alexander, in April 1917.

❧ III ❧
WARFARE

❦

You cannot make a revolution with silk gloves.
  Joseph Stalin

❦

World War One broke out in August 1914 with the assassination in Sarajevo of Austria-Hungary's Archduke Franz Ferdi-
nand. Due to a complicated web of pacts and treaties, the
countries of Europe declared war on one another and the
hostilities began in earnest. Russia entered the war on the
side of the Allies.

REVOLUTION DURING YEARS
OF WAR

꧁꧂

S talin and other Bolsheviks were drafted into the army in October 1916, and he arrived at Krasnoyarsk in February 1917 for deployment. He was declared unfit for duty because of his disabled left arm, and because he still had four months of exile to serve, he was sent to nearby Achinsk. In St. Petersburg, the February Revolution forced Nicholas II from power, and the Tsar abdicated the throne. Monarchy was replaced by a provisional government.

꧁꧂

STALIN RETURNED TO ST. PETERSBURG, now called Petrograd, and resumed editorial control of *Pravda* alongside fellow Bolshevik Lev Kamenev. He was appointed as the Bolshevik representative to the Executive Committee of the Petrograd Soviet, a council of the city's workers, and in April 1917, the Bolshevik Central Committee elections resulted in the top three officers being Lenin, Zinoviev and Stalin. His position in the leadership of the Bolshevik Party was cemented.

❧

HE ORGANIZED the July Days uprising, which was a show of strength by the Bolsheviks. The uprising was suppressed by the provisional government, which began to crack down on the Bolsheviks and raided the offices of *Pravda*. During the chaos of the government backlash, Stalin took control of security for Lenin and smuggled him out of Petrograd to Razliv, where he could remain in hiding.

❧

WITH LENIN ON THE RUN, Stalin served as the de facto head of the Bolsheviks, and he called a covert Sixth Congress. Lenin called on the Bolsheviks to overthrow the provisional government, something that Stalin and Leo Trotsky soundly supported. Kamenev opposed the idea until Lenin returned to Petrograd and convinced them to act.

RED OCTOBER

❀

On October 24, 1917, the provisional government again raided *Pravda* and smashed its printing presses. The next day, Stalin and Lenin met with the Central Committee at Smolny Institute. From there, they oversaw the October Revolution. In later years, Trotsky tried to discredit Stalin by minimizing his role, but Stalin was a senior member of the Central Committee and certainly played a part in the direction of the revolution.

❀

LENIN FORMED a new government on October 26, 1917, the Council of People's Commissars (Sovnarkom), of which Lenin himself was chairman. Stalin supported Lenin's choice not to ally with the Mensheviks, although the Bolsheviks did form a coalition with the Left Socialist Revolutionaries. When the dust settled, four men were in control of the government:

Lenin, Stalin, Trotsky and Yakov Sverdlov. The four became three when Sverdlov died in March 1919.

☙❧

THE BOLSHEVIKS BEGAN to suppress all opposition through mass killings and political repression during what is called the Red Terror. During this time, Stalin co-signed Lenin's decrees shutting down hostile newspapers and was instrumental in the creation of the Cheka, the Bolshevik secret police. He co-authored the constitution of the new Russian Soviet Federative Socialist Republic with Sverdlov.

☙❧

HE WAS APPOINTED the People's Commissar for Nationalities, and in November 1917 he issued the Decree on Nationality that gave ethnic and national minorities the right to secession and self-determination. He traveled to Helsinki and promised independence to the Finnish Social Democrats, which was granted in December 1917. Some members of the party accused him of pushing national self-determination as a smoke screen to conceal Sovnarkom's imperialist policies, but this accusation gained no traction.

☙❧

HE HIRED a secretary nave Nadezhda Alliluyeva, the daughter of one of the Bolshevik party faithful and his long-time friend, Sergei Alliluyev. The two were married in 1919.

☙❧

IN MARCH 1918, the Bolsheviks moved the capital from

Petrograd to Moscow, and Stalin took apartments in the Kremlin. Lenin, with Stalin's support, signed an armistice with the Central Powers that allowed Russia to exit the World War. The Treaty of Brest-Litovsk cost Russia a great deal of territory but allowed the Bolsheviks to concentrate on domestic matters instead of the foreign war. The Left Socialist Revolutionaries left the coalition government in protest over the loss of territory. The Bolsheviks were now the only group in charge.

CIVIL WAR

✦

The Bolsheviks soon found themselves opposed by both right wing and left-wing armies, and the Russian Civil War began. Stalin was sent to Tsaritsyn in May 1918 to secure the food supply, and when he got there, he took command of the military forces in the area. He met and befriended fellow Bolsheviks Kliment Voroshilov and Semyon Budyonny, who would be his staunchest military and political supporters from then on.

✦

STALIN WAS a believer in victory through superior numbers, and as a result, he sent a large body of Red Army troops against the White Russians, who were tsarists. The Red Army took heavy losses, but the White Russians were defeated. He would carry this philosophy with him into the future.

✦

WHILE IN TSARITSYN, Stalin began to display some of the tactics and methods that would make him infamous. He began to execute counter-revolutionaries, often without trials, and he purged the military and food-collection agencies of all middle-class specialists. Some were even executed, again without trials, and against Lenin's orders. He ruthlessly enforced compliance with his rules by torching several villages as object lessons in obedience.

❧

IN DECEMBER 1918, he drew up decrees recognizing the Marxist Soviet republics in Estonia, Lithuania and Latvia. These Baltic nations declared independence from Russia, but Stalin refused to allow them to leave. He ignored and discredited these declarations of independence.

❧

IN DECEMBER 1918, he traveled to Perm to lead an inquiry into a devastating defeat of the Red Army by the White Russians led by Alexander Kolchak. When he learned in March 1919 that the Third Regiment of the army on the Western Front had defected, he ordered any captured defectors to be publicly shot.

❧

FOR HIS EFFORTS, he was awarded the Order of the Red Banner in November 1919, and in 1920 he was named head of the Workers' and Peasant's Inspectorate. In 1921, he met his son Yakov and brought him back to Moscow, where Stalin's wife Nadezhda had given birth to another son, Vassily, that month.

THE POLISH-SOVIET WAR

❦

I n early 1920, warfare with Poland erupted, and Stalin was moved to Ukraine. The Polish Army invaded Russia, and the Red Army pushed the Poles back into Poland. Stalin became obsessed with taking the city of Lwów, and he concentrated his forces on that target to the extent the he even disobeyed orders to send reinforcements to fellow Red Army commander Mikhail Tukhachevsky.

❦

THE RED ARMY COUNTERATTACKED POLAND, but in August 1920, the Poles repulsed the Soviet advance. Stalin was recalled to Moscow, and a peace treaty was signed. The defeat by Poland was an embarrassment. Stalin and Trotsky blamed each other for the failure to take Poland and to encourage the Polish proletariat to rise up. Stalin was angry about the way that the war had been fought, and he demanded to be released from the military. This request was granted.

᭰᭰

AT THE 9TH BOLSHEVIK CONFERENCE, Stalin stood accused of insubordination and military incompetence based on his failure to support Tukhachevsky. In public speeches, Trotsky blamed Stalin for "strategic mistakes". The entire affair was bruising for Stalin's ego.

NATIONALISM

※

Stalin believed that ethnic minorities, like Georgians, should have limited autonomy within the Russian state. Georgia, like other small countries in the former Russian Empire who had been forcibly Sovietized, wished to have complete autonomy from Moscow.

※

THE ARGUMENT CAME to a head when Lenin stated his intention to mesh all of the nations of the Caucasus into one entity, the Transcaucasian Socialist Federative Soviet Republic. Georgia specifically opposed this and pushed for full-member status within the Russian state. The Georgian Bolsheviks pushing for Georgian autonomy were Filipp Makharadze and Budu Mdivani. They were directly opposed by Stalin and his cohort, Grigori Ordzhonikidze.

※

ACCORDING to the Communist Manifesto of Karl Marx, there were no countries, only workers combined in their struggle against the bourgeoisie. The recognition of individual countries brought scorn from Marxists in Moscow, and because of his intention to allow ethnic minorities limited autonomy, Stalin was labeled "un-Marxist" and in league with nationalists.

☙❧

A POWER STRUGGLE erupted in Georgia. It mimicked the power struggle that was going on in Moscow around the ailing Lenin. Georgian Bolshevik leadership courted Lenin, hoping that he would come to support their cause, but Lenin's illness was distracting him from matters of state. He disagreed with Stalin's tactics, which were to strong-arm the local Menshevik majority, but he did not officially support the Georgian cause.

☙❧

STALIN, working within his power as a senior member of the Central Committee, removed Makharadze from power and replaced him with men who were more in line with Stalin's attitudes. A Mdivani representative and Ordzhonikidze came to blows over the matter, and the Georgian Central Executive Committee sent a list of grievances to Lenin, hoping to finally woo him to their side.

☙❧

LENIN SENT BACK a statement supporting Stalin. The moderate communist government in Georgia was swept away, replaced with Bolshevik hard-liners who were in Stalin's pocket. In 1923, the Politburo did away with Mdivani and Georgia was forced into the amalgamated soviet republic it had wanted to avoid, with Ordzhonikidze at the helm.

❧

WHILE ALL THIS was going on, peasant strikes and workers' protests spread across Russia in opposition to Sovnarkom's food requisitioning program. Alarmed by the prospect of his regime being toppled, Lenin agreed to economic reforms called the New Economic Policy (NEP). In the debates over this policy, Trotsky pushed for the abolition of trade unions, which Lenin and Stalin fiercely opposed.

❧

STALIN GATHERED power within the party and began to push out Trotsky, the third man in the Central Committee leadership. As Lenin's health continued to fail, and as Stalin more and more controlled who contacted the leader and for what reason, his advantage over his rival became nearly absolute.

CLOSING THE FIST

৩১৩

S talin was named as the supervisor of the Department of Agitation and Propaganda within the Central Committee, and at the 11ᵗʰ Party Congress in 1922, Lenin nominated him as General Secretary. There were concerns that this appointment would make Stalin too powerful, but he was put into the office despite those arguments.

৩১৩

LENIN CONTINUED TO FAIL, and Stalin continued to control his communications with Sovnarkom. His stranglehold on communication with Lenin angered Nadezhda Krupskaya, and the two had a heated exchange via telephone. When Lenin learned of Stalin's rudeness to his wife, his opinion of his Georgian counterpart slipped, and he began to write notes suggesting that Stalin should be removed as General Secretary. These notes were never delivered, but they were gathered together into his Testament.

❧

THE USSR WAS FORMED and ratified in December 1922. It ostensibly had a constitution and equal rights of determination among all of the states beneath its umbrella, but all the true power was in the hands of the Politburo of the Communist Party of the Soviet Union in Moscow – and Stalin controlled the Politburo.

❧

LENIN DIED IN JANUARY 1924, and Stalin wasted no time in positioning himself as mourner in chief. Lenin's body was embalmed and put on display in a mausoleum in Red Square, over the objections of his wife. The cult of personality went into high gear, and Petrograd was renamed Leningrad in the late leader's honor. Stalin presented himself as a dedicated Leninist, even going so far as to give lectures on Leninism at Sverdlov University. His lectures were compiled and published as a book.

❧

AT THE 13TH PARTY CONGRESS, Lenin's Testimony was read aloud. It excoriated Stalin, who was so deeply embarrassed that he offered to resign. Because of his "humility," he was allowed to keep his position.

❧

LENIN HAD DIED without naming a successor, and the struggle to replace him was vicious. Stalin formed an anti-Trotsky coalition with Kamenev and Zinoviev, while Trotsky led the Left Opposition, criticizing the NEP. Stalin built up the Central Committee with people he knew to be loyal to him, and soon the Left Opposition was forced out. The Right Opposition, led by Nikolai Bukharin, now supported Stalin. Trotsky would not gain power.

※

IN LATE 1924, Stalin removed supporters of Kamenev and Zinoviev from positions of authority, and by 1925 the line was clearly drawn with Stalin and Bukharin on one side and Kamenev and Zinoviev on the other. They bickered publicly at the 14th Party Congress, and the bad blood deepened.

※

IN MID-1926, Kamenev, Zinoviev and Trotsky joined forced as the United Opposition against Stalin. Under duress and facing threats of expulsion from Russia, Kamenev and Zinoviev both recanted their criticisms of Stalin. The reversal was not enough to keep Zinoviev in Stalin's good graces, and in October 1928, Zinoviev and Trotsky were removed from the Central Committee. Trotsky was exiled to Khazakhstan, then deported completely in 1929.

※

THE CENTRAL COMMITTEE was now made up entirely of Stalin loyalists. The four men in power, after Stalin himself, were Vyacheslav Molotov, the head of government; Kliment

Voroshilov; Lazar Kaganovich; and Sergo Ordzhonikedze from Georgia. There was no one to oppose him now.

❧

IN 1924, Georgian nationalists launched the August Uprising, which was put down by the Red Army. As a signal of his victory, Tsaritsyn was renamed Stalingrad, a city that would soon gain notoriety it never wanted.

❧ IV ❧
PURGES

❁

Education is a weapon whose effects depend on who holds it in his hands and at whom it is aimed.
    Joseph Stalin

❁

In 1927, Stalin turned against Lenin's New Economic Policy. The USSR still lagged behind Western Europe, grain production was down, and he fears invasion from the increasingly militarized Japan, France and United Kingdom. He needed to strengthen his position and his nation.

❁

Hard-line communists held that the NEP was too capitalist

in nature, and they strongly disliked the men who were profiting from it, the affluent peasants (kulaks) and the small business owners (Nepmen).

❦

In the face of looming food shortages, Stalin traveled to Novosibirsk, where he accused the kulaks of hoarding grain. He had the kulaks arrested and all of their grain hauled back to Moscow. Violent "grain procurement squads" were sent out across Western Siberia and the Ural Mountain region. Stalin announced that kulaks and "middle peasants" would be forced to share their grain on pain of arrest or death. Bukharin opposed this policy, feeling it was too harsh and too rash. As always, Stalin ignored the nay-sayers. He only heard what he wanted to hear.

❦

In January 1930, the Politburo approved a measure to liquidate the kulaks. This entire class of people were rounded up and either exiled or sent to concentration camps in Siberia. Many died en route. By July, more than 350,000 had lost everything through his program of "dekulakization".

COLLECTIVE FARMS AND
DISSATISFACTION

⚜

In 1929, the Politburo announced mass collectivization of agriculture, forming *kolkhozy*, collective farms, and *sovkhoz*, state farms. Kulaks were banned from joining these collectives, but other peasants were "encouraged" to join up. Many did so out of fear of reprisal, giving up their family land and homes. Production slumped along with morale.

⚜

FAMINE FELL upon the Russian people, and the Politburo attempted to redistribute food to the worst-hit areas, but the task was too large and they were unable to give the people enough to eat.

⚜

ARMED PEASANT UPRISINGS broke out in Ukraine, the

northern Caucasus, southern Russia and central Asia. They were broken by the Red Army. Stalin blamed the unrest on local officials and continued to press for collectivization. Bukharin opposed this policy, and he was removed from the Politburo for his trouble in November 1929.

⚬⚬⚬

STALIN ATTEMPTED to plan the economy using policies based upon short-term goals. The first five-year plan focused on heavy industry, determined to build up the manufacturing sector of the Russian economy. The plan achieved all of its objectives a year early, in 1932. The USSR began to boom with new mines, new cities and a new canal (White Sea/Baltic). Peasants streamed into the city to participate, and urban housing was ill equipped to deal with the influx of people.

⚬⚬⚬

THE SURGE in manufacturing came at a cost, and the USSR built up heavy foreign debts through purchasing industrial machinery from overseas. It was decided that these debts would be paid off using the export of grain from the USSR's farms, which left even less food in the coffers for the people.

⚬⚬⚬

NOT ALL OF the workers who came to the city did so voluntarily. Many of the major infrastructure projects that were completed during this period were created using forced labor. Workers lost control over their industries, and factory managers began to enjoy privileges and perks. Wage disparities were colossal, but Stalin defended these by pointing out

Marx's own argument that such wage gaps were necessary in the early phases of socialism.

❧

DESPITE ALL OF THESE PROBLEMS, Stalin presented a Utopian vision of the socialist state, and as defense of his assertions, he pointed to the 1929 stock market crash as proof that capitalism was doomed. He declared that class war between the proletariat and their enemies would grow as socialism matured, and he warned of right-wing threats within the Communist party. He began to see conspiracies and enemies everywhere he looked.

SHOW TRIALS AND THE SOVIET STYLE

꧁꧂

The first major show trial of Stalin's scapegoats was the Shakhty Trial in 1928. A group of middle-class "industrial specialists" stood accused of sabotage. Fifty-three people stood accused, and all were convicted. Five were sentenced to death and the rest were imprisoned. One of those killed, Nikolai Karlovich von Meck (nephew by marriage of the composer Tchaikovsky), was accused of "wrecking" the railroads. Wrecking became a capital crime. Workers who did not produce as much as the party believed they should were accused of working with capitalist elements to undermine the socialist system, and they were tried, imprisoned, and sometimes executed. Through 1929 and 1930, more show trials took place, designed both to eliminate political rivals and to intimidate the opposition.

꧁꧂

STALIN BEGIN to promote ethnic Russians to positions of authority all throughout the country, and the Russian language was made compulsory everywhere in the USSR. Ethnic groups' nationalism was harshly suppressed.

⚜

IN ADDITION to his Russification projects, Stalin also instituted conservative social policies that were aimed at increasing social discipline and increasing the Soviet population. There was an emphasis on family and motherhood, and homosexuality was re-criminalized. Limits were placed on abortion and *Zhenotdel*, the section of the Secretariat of the Communist Party that dealt with women's issues.

⚜

FORMERLY "ELITE" culture – ballet, opera, poetry – was disseminated more widely throughout the country, no doubt spurred by Stalin's own interest in these same things. He pushed for improved universal education in the arts and sciences, as long as what was taught conformed with his own views. "Socialist realism" was encouraged across the arts. This is a form of art that glorifies socialist ideals using realistic imagery, usually within set confines of what is and what is not acceptable. Dissident art was not tolerated.

⚜

PERHAPS AS A REACTION to his years of enforced religious schooling, Stalin instituted a virulent anti-religion campaign. He increased funding for the League of Militant Atheists, and Christian, Jewish, Muslin and Buddhist clergy were all harshly persecuted. Churches were pulled down all across the USSR. The most striking example is the Cathedral of Christ the Savior in Moscow, which was destroyed to make room for the Palace of the Soviets – which was never completed.

TROUBLE AT HOME

☙❦❧

As Stalin's power grew, his home life became more unsteady. While he was preoccupied with decrying enemies of the state, real and imagined, his family was coming apart.

☙❦❧

YAKOV ATTEMPTED SUICIDE IN 1929. His father responded with scorn and contempt, making it clear that Yakov should have succeeded if he'd wanted to earn Stalin's respect. Stalin considered the suicide attempt to be blackmail and joked that his son couldn't even shoot straight.

☙❦❧

STALIN'S MARRIAGE WAS STORMY, with frequent yelling matches. Both Stalin and Nadezhda were temperamental, but her irritability was exacerbated by frequent headaches and a possible case of manic depression. The couple had three children – Vassily, Svetlana, and Artyom, whom they had adopted – but Stalin was distant and frequently harsh. He had a habit of womanizing in front of her, and in November 1932, he ignored Nadezhda in favor of flirting with the young wives of his revolutionary officers. Disgruntled and overtaken by her mental illness, Nadezhda shot herself to death.

※※※

STALIN WAS INCONSOLABLE. He threatened suicide, and he turned his bitter grief into hatred of the world, blaming everyone at the party for the sorrow that had driven his beloved wife to suicide. In the days after her death, his emotions seemed to shut down, leaving no trace of compassion behind. That compassion, the little that he'd had, never returned.

TROUBLE IN THE FIELDS

꧁꧂

I n May 1932, there was such a level off social unrest in the country that Stalin agreed to loosen his economic policies enough for *kolkhoz* markets to be established, where peasants could trade their surplus produce. The surpluses were few and far between. Criminal penalties became harsher and more severe, as in August 1932, the theft of a handful of grain was named a capital crime.

꧁꧂

THE SECOND FIVE-YEAR economic plan that Stalin devised was aimed at improving living conditions and the production of household goods. The factories filled with workers, all of whom needed to be fed.

꧁꧂

GRAIN WAS TAKEN from the fields in Ukraine where it was

grown and shipped wholesale to the cities. Little to nothing was left behind. Famine gripped the northern Caucasus and Ukraine in the winter of 1932-1933, mostly due to Stalin's policies regarding redistribution of grain. The effects of the hunger were catastrophic. Between five million and seven million people starved to death, many of them in Ukraine. Thousands resorted to cannibalism to survive. Stalin refused to accept that his policies had anything to do with the famine, choosing instead to blame counter-revolutionaries, wreckers in the fields, and the peasants themselves.

⚅⚄⚅

THE FAMINE WAS CONCEALED from foreign observers with subterfuge and outright denial. Today this period is known in Ukraine as Holodomor and is considered genocide by the Soviet government against ethnic Ukrainians. Some have postulated that Stalin in fact did not deliberately starve the people of the Ukraine, but it cannot be denied that he certainly did nothing to help them.

FOREIGN AFFAIRS

In 1934, the USSR joined the League of Nations. When Hitler was elected German Chancellor, he and Stalin exchanged friendly correspondence. Stalin admired Hitler as a man of strength and action, but he did not trust him, and he was wary of the threat of fascism. After Hitler's inauguration, Stalin ordered many factories to shift from building household goods to building armaments.

STALIN SIGNED a treaty of mutual assistance with France and Czechoslovakia, and in 1936, a new constitution was released, but all of its promises and tenets were hollow. All power remained in the hands of the Politburo, and the Politburo answered to Stalin alone.

THE COMMUNIST INTERNATIONAL Seventh Congress in July – August 1935 issued a statement encouraging Marxists and Leninists around the world to come together in a united front against fascism. In response, Germany, Fascist Italy and Japan signed the Anit-Comintern (Communist International) Pact of 1935.

ॐ

THE SPANISH CIVIL War erupted in 1936, with right-wing Nationalists on one side, backed by Germany and Italy, and left-wing Republicans, backed by the USSR. Three thousand Soviet trooped traveled to Spain to assist with the revolution, but despite their efforts, the Nationalists won the day. Fascism had scored its first victory over Marxism.

❧ V ☙

THE GREAT TERROR

⁂

The death of one man is a tragedy. The death of millions is a statistic.

Joseph Stalin

⁂

Stalin gave mixed signals in 1933 and 1934. He released minor criminals from prison with amnesty and ordered the authorities to stop conducting mass arrests and deportations. He also ordered the Politburo to investigate false imprisonment. At the same time, he ordered the arrest and execution of workers at the Stalin Metallurgical Factory, who were accused of spying for Japan. With one hand he was meting out justice and clemency, and with the other hand he searched out enemies of the state virtually everywhere.

TIPPING POINT

Senior party member Sergey Kirov was assassinated in December 1934. Leonid Nikolayev entered Kirov's offices at Smolny Institute and shot him in the back of the neck. At the time, Kirov had only four NKVD (secret police) body guards, who only accompanied him to his office. They had left the scene before Nikolayev arrived. The assassin was arrested quickly, and on December 29, 1934, he was sentenced to death. He was shot to death that night. Commissar Borisov, the only other person present at the assassination, died the day after the assassination, "accidentally" falling from a moving truck filled with NKVD officers. Nikolayev's family and friends were arrested and sent to labor camps, usually without benefit of a trial. His wife was executed.

NIKOLAYEV, under direct interrogation by Stalin himself,

confessed to being as assassin in the pay of a fascist power, and that he was one of many who were seeking to undermine the Soviet Union. Immediately after this dubious confession, 104 people who were already in prison and who could not have been involved in the assassination plot were nonetheless found guilty of collusion and summarily executed.

๑๛๏

SUDDENLY EVERYONE WAS SUSPECT. Stalin became obsessed with his own personal safety and prioritized his own security above all else. He began to purge the Central Committee, and all opposition members were imprisoned. Opposition leaders who were already in prison were charged with new crimes and shot.

๑๛๏

IN 1935, the NKVD were empowered to run "troikas", small units of three officers each who could act as judge, jury and executioner as they saw fit. The secret police were ordered to expel suspected counter-revolutionaries, especially those who had been aristocrats, landlords or business owners before the October Revolution. In Leningrad alone, 11,000 people were eliminated.

BOILING OVER

❦

More show trials began. In August 1936, Stalin's former Bolshevik colleagues Kamenev and Zinoviev were accused of plotting to assassinate Stalin, and they were convicted and executed. Another show trial followed in January 1937, and a third in March 1938 saw old Bolsheviks Bukharin and Rykov standing trial for involvement in a pro-Trotsky terrorist plot. They were executed. By late 1937, through show trials and mass expulsions from the party, all traces of opposition opinions had been purged from the Politburo, and all power rested in Stalin's hands alone.

❦

AS THE LEADER of the global Marxist movement, Stalin commanded communist parties in other countries to begin expelling anti-Stalinists. The NKVD began to commit assassinations abroad under direct orders from Stalin himself. One of these assassinations was Leo Trotsky, who was shot to death in Mexico in August 1940. He was the last of Stalin's old opponents to die.

❧

THE PURGE ELIMINATED all political dissent. The old party members were swept away and replaced with young, dedicated Stalinists who had never known a different leader. They were eager to please, and they performed their parts of the purge with a will, sometimes exceeding their stated quotas of apprehended spies and enemies of the state. If Stalin was dangerous, the people who killed to stay on his good side were worse.

❧

ONCE ALL OF his political enemies had been destroyed, Stalin shifted the attention of his purge to the citizenry at large. Between December 1936 and November 1938, the Great Purge swept away all "anti-Soviet" elements: Bolsheviks who had opposed him, Mensheviks, members of the Socialist Revolutionary party, priests, White Army soldiers, and common criminals. With Nikolai Yezhov, the head of the NKVD, Stalin signed Order No. 00447, which listed 268,950 "enemies of the state". All were arrested, and of this number, 75,950 were executed.

❧

STALIN BEGAN TO PURSUE "NATIONAL OPERATIONS" designed to ethnically cleanse the USSR of "inferior" ethnic groups, like the Poles, Germans, Latvians, Finns, Greeks, Koreans and Chinese. They were either internally exiled or deported. In all, 1.6 million people were arrested, and at least 700,000 were shot. It's not known how many people died under NKVD torture.

☙❧

STALIN PERSONALLY DIRECTED all of it. He took a keen interest in the details of the deaths and confessions of these enemies of the state. His paranoia reached new heights, and anyone could be a conspirator or a potential assassin. Foreign opinion began to turn against Stalin as a result of the Great Purge, even as Germany was clearly building up for hostile action. Fearing that he would be left alone to face the German army if was should come, Stalin made one last sacrifice on the altar of socialism. In April 1939, Yezhov was arrested, and he was executed in 1940. Stalin blamed all of the excesses of the Purge on the now conveniently silenced NKVD director. He could try to deflect the shadow, but the Purge had severely damaged his standing with leftist groups abroad.

THE GREAT PATRIOTIC
WAR

᭥

I trust no one, not even myself.
  Joseph Stalin

᭥

Stalin was not surprised when the Second World War began in 1939. He had been expecting hostilities from Germany and Japan long before that year, with most of his concern being focused to the east. He had entered into a sort of pen pal relationship with Hitler, and he felt that they understood one another. It was his hope that while he was dealing with Japan, his good German friend would overwhelm France and the UK, leaving Russia the dominant power in Europe.

᭥

He had hope for a war in which the USSR could benefit without fighting. He remembered the disaster that had been Russia's involvement in the First World War, and he had no wish to repeat them. He tried to remain neutral. All the same, the Red Army more than doubled in the years from 1939 to 1941. As the saying goes, just because you're paranoid, it doesn't mean you don't have enemies.

A NEUTRAL RUSSIA

❧

When tentative offers of alliance with France and the UK were met with rejection, Stalin reached out to Germany. The two countries began to negotiate terms of a treaty in May 1939, a document that proposed diving Eastern Europe between them. A non-aggression pact was signed with Germany in August 1939, and exactly one week later, the Wehrmacht rolled into Poland. The UK and France declared war on Germany, and the conflict was begun.

❧

ON SEPTEMBER 17, 1939, the Red Army invaded eastern Poland, alleging to the outside world that its intentions were to "restore order" near its territory. More horse trading with Germany followed, and more territory was exchanged. In return for ceding western Poland to Germany, Lithuania and the Baltic states were granted to the USSR. This German-

Soviet Frontier Treaty was signed in Stalin's presence on September 28, 1939. Germany and the USSR began to trade, which undermined Britain's blockade.

❧

THE BALTIC STATES, which had attempted to declare their freedom from the Soviet Union, were forcefully annexed in August 1939. They attempted to also annex Finland through an invasion called the Winter War, but the determined Finns held off the Soviet advance despite inferior numbers. The defeat embarrassed Stalin. As a result of the failed invasion, the USSR was expelled from the League of Nations, and it was formed to sign and the Moscow Peace Treaty with Finland. To console himself, Stalin ordered the annexation of Bessarabia and Bukovina, provinces in Romania, in June 1940.

❧

ONCE THE SOVIETS OCCUPIED A TERRITORY, they wasted no time before cracking down on any signs of dissent. The most egregious of these crack-downs was what came to be known as the Katyn Massacre. In April and May 1940, over 22,000 Polish soldiers, police officers and intelligentsia were shot to death by the NKVD and buried in a mass grave in a Polish forest. The German Army discovered the mass grave in 1943, but the Soviets insisted that Germany was responsible. Russia continued to deny responsibility until 1990 when declassified documents pertaining to the massacre were released.

❧

ON THE WESTERN FRONT, Stalin was shocked by the speed with which the Nazis toppled France. He knew that it was only a matter of time before the Germans pivoted back toward the east and Russia. Attempting to forestall the inevitable for as long as possible, he attempted to appease Hitler to buy time. On September 27, 1940, he signed the Tri-Partite Pact along with the Axis Powers (Germany, Italy and Japan). He floated the idea of Russia joining the Axis in October 1940, but he was rebuffed. They were suspicious of his motives. In an effort to prove his good intentions, he signed a neutrality pact with Japan in April 1941.

৩৯৩

HE KNEW WAR WAS COMING, and he was determined to have control over how the Soviet Union responded. He dismissed Molotov and took the position of Premier of the Soviet Union on May 6, 1941. His dictatorship was now complete.

WITH FRIENDS LIKE THESE...

❧

I n June 1941, Germany invaded the USSR. Despite his conviction that war was coming, Stalin was still surprised by the timing. In response, he formed the Supreme Command (Stavka) and the State Committee of Defense.

❧

THE GERMAN BLITZKRIEG was initially very successful, taking all of the Baltic States, Ukraine and Belorussia in short order. Refugees flooded to Moscow and Leningrad, but some Soviet citizens, those who had suffered under the Soviet system, saw the Germans as liberators. The Germans saw them as subhuman (üntermensch) and suitable only for slave labor. Their misery continued.

❧

IN JULY 1941, the Luftwaffe began bombing Moscow, and the Wehrmacht began preparing an all-out assault on the Soviet capital. The Soviet government made arrangements to flee to the relative safety of Kuibyshev, but Stalin was determined to stay in Moscow to preserve troop morale.

❧

AS WITH NAPOLEON A CENTURY BEFORE, the Germans had not counted on the Russian secret weapon: winter. The Germans were inadequately prepared, and their uniforms were insufficient for the rigors of biting cold. Machinery malfunctioned, travel became impossible, and soldiers froze to death within sight of the spires of Moscow. Faced with total annihilation by the forces of Nature, the Germans retreated.

... WHO NEEDS ENEMIES?

꧁꧂

In response to the German invasion, Stalin ordered a scorched earth policy. Food stuffs, villages, bridges and towns were burned before the enemy could reach them. In addition, based on fear of collaborators – a fear that had already informed much of the Great Purge – he ordered the NKVD to kill 100,000 political prisoners in areas close to the German advance. Military command was also scoured of any hint of rebellion or opposition.

꧁꧂

As proof of his determination, he issued Order No. 270, which ordered any soldier facing capture to commit suicide or fight to the death. It was declared that any soldier who allowed himself to be taken prisoner would be considered a traitor. One such "traitor" was Stalin's unlucky son Yakov, who was taken by the Germans and later died in Sachsenhausen Concentration Camp when he was shot in the head by a sentry. Another order, Order No. 227, was issued in July 1942, and it declared that any soldier retreating from battle would be put into penal battalions and used as cannon fodder.

෮෯෨

IN 1941, the USSR allied with the UK, France, and later with the USA. Help in dealing with the German invasion didn't arrive until 1942. By then, all Soviet resources had been thrown into military production.

෮෯෨

STALIN MAY HAVE HAD an iron fist, but he understood that morale was vital in war time. He began to tolerate the Russian Orthodox Church more than before, and he even met with Patriarch Sergius, the leader of the Church, in September 1943. He allowed formerly suppressed writers and artists, like Anna Akhmatova and Dmitri Shostakovich, to distribute and perform their works. He also commissioned a new, more patriotic national anthem. He dissolved ComIntern in 1943 to allay Winston Churchill's fears of a spread of communism, and he sponsored the Jewish Anti-Fascist Committee to garner more Jewish and foreign support for the Russian war effort.

STALINGRAD

༺❀༻

I n May 1942, the Red Army launched an unsuccessful counterattack against the Germans in Kharkov, Ukraine. Soviet forces led by Marshal Semyon Timoshenko attacked the Germans from a salient the Red Army had forced when they'd repelled the Germans from Moscow in the winter. Timoshenko and other Soviet leaders, including Stalin, believed too much in the abilities of their troops and woefully underestimated the German will to fight. The counterattack was hit hard by air strikes and a messy retreat allowed the Germans to form a pincer that encircled 250,000 Soviet soldiers, who were mowed down by attack from all sides. In the end, over 70,000 Soviets were killed and 240,000 taken prisoner, compared to 20,000 German casualties.

༺❀༻

AFTER KHARKOV, the Germans shifted their attention south, toward Russian oil fields. Stalin believed incorrectly that this was a feint to led the Red Army away from its defense of Moscow. Instead, the German Army attacked Stalingrad.

STALIN ORDERED that the town that shared his name should be held at any costs. He would take it as a personal defeat if the city were to surrender. Hitler, who knew something about the ego of his opponent, put just as much pressure on taking it. It was a dictator's fistfight carried out by proxy.

THE BATTLE RAGED FOR MONTHS, from August 23, 1942 to February 2, 1943. The opening attack saw the Luftwaffe reducing the majority of the city to rubble. There was desperate hand-to-hand battle in the streets as the armies fought from house to house. The Luftwaffe continued bombing civilian targets, and the Soviets fought with incredible determination to hold the city.

WHEN 91,000 STARVING German troops finally surrendered and were taken prisoner, the Germans had drawn so many reinforcements from the western front that they were never able to recover. The German defeat, coupled with the massive expenditures devoted to taking Stalingrad in the dictators' grudge match, was a turning point in the war that inevitably led to Nazi Germany's downfall.

IN RECOGNITION OF THE VICTORY, Stalingrad was recognized with the title Hero City in 1945, and Stalin declared himself Marshal of the Soviet Union.

COUNTER-ATTACK

☙❦❧

The Red Army began a fierce counter attack in November 1942 and stayed on the offensive for the rest of the war. There were battles won, and the Germans were distracted from the western front, which eased pressure on the other Allied armies. There were good feelings toward Stalin in the West, and in 1942 he was named *Time* Magazine's Man of the Year. When he learned that some westerners (mostly Americans) were affectionately calling him "Uncle Joe," he was deeply offended at the disrespect.

☙❦❧

THE EFFORT of keeping Germany on its toes on the eastern front cost the Soviets dearly. Bu the end of the war, there were nearly 2.5 million Soviet casualties, the most of any of the Allies.

☙❦❧

DESPITE THE PUBLIC'S affection for Stalin, there were still lingering suspicions between the leaders of the Allies (Churchill, Stalin and Roosevelt). In November 1943, at a meeting of the Big Three in Tehran, a site of Stalin's choosing, they agreed upon the apportionment of the world after the war, particularly with regard to Germany and Eastern Europe. Stalin pressed for and was granted the German city of Konigsberg, as well as for Bulgaria, Hungary, Romania and Yugoslavia. Those countries' futures were happily signed away.

❦

BEGINNING IN 1944, Germany began losing ground to the Red Army. They were pushed out of the Baltic States, which were re-annexed by the USSR. The next territories taken by the Red Army were the Caucasus and Crimea, where the ethnic groups there were accused of being collaborators with the Germans and were punished by losing their right to autonomous republics. Nearly a million of these ethnic minorities were internally exiled to Siberia.

❦

IN 1945, the Big Three met again in the resort town of Yalta. Again, they discussed the apportionment of the globe in utter disregard of the wishes of the people already residing in those places. The UK and the USA agreed that Germany should be forced to pay $20 billion in reparations, and that the USSR should be given the Sakhalin and Kurile Islands in return for entering the war against Japan.

❦

STALIN SECRETLY HAD designs on Poland. When the Poles asked the USSR for help in the Warsaw Uprising, he purposefully withheld it, hoping that the resulting strain would encourage the Polish proletariat to rise up and establish a Marxist state. He also worried that successful freedom fighters would bolster the Polish people against efforts to bring Poland under the USSR's mantle.

☙❦❧

WHEN IT CAME to Berlin itself, Stalin wanted to take the city in order to expand his Marxist agenda. Roosevelt didn't see this hidden aim, but Churchill read it plainly. Despite all of his efforts, Churchill was unable to persuade Roosevelt to make a priority of reaching Berlin before the Soviets.

❧ VII ❧
VICTORY AND AFTERMATH

❧

Death is the solution to all problems. No man – no problem.

Joseph Stalin

❧

In April 1945, the Red Army took Berlin, and on hearing the news, Hitler committed suicide. Stalin was put out by this, because he had wanted to capture Hitler and bring him back to Moscow alive. He did the next best thing and ordered his intelligence officers to bring Hitler's corpse to Moscow instead, like some sort of trophy of war.

❧

When Soviet troops discovered the first of the Nazi death camps, they responded by looting, raping and pillaging the German population. Stalin refused to punish the offenders, stating that such outlets of tension were only natural in men who had been subjected to the horrors of war.

THE DAWN OF THE ATOMIC AGE

๛

T he Allies' attention switched to defeating Japan. Stalin was well aware that the US had constructed an atomic bomb, and he was determined to occupy the land he had been given at Yalta before the Americans could get there.

๛

ON AUGUST 6, 1945, the Americans dropped the first atomic bomb in human history on Hiroshima, Japan. Stalin took advantage of the ensuing chaos by invading Japanese-occupied Manchuria on August 8. On August 9, the second atomic bomb was dropped on Nagasaki, and Japan surrendered.

๛

WHEN THE ALLIES moved in to occupy Japan, Stalin wanted to assist by occupying half of the country. The Americans refused to allow this and occupied the entire nation before Stalin's troops could arrive.

⁂

THE BIG THREE met in July and August 1945 for the Potsdam Conference. Stalin attended, along with British Prime Minister Clement Atlee and American President Harry S. Truman. At the conference, he promised not to "Sovietize" eastern Europe, with no intention of keeping that promise. He demanded reparations that were far in excess of the German people's ability to pay, and he pushed for "war booty" – the right to seize property from conquered countries without limitation. A clause was inserted allowing war booty, with some limitations. Berlin was divided into four parts, each to be governed by a different power (US, UK, France and USSR).

RETURN TO NORMAL

☙❧

I n June 1945, he added "Generalissimus" to his titles, and he openly praised ethnic Russians above all other ethnic groups for the first time. The accusations of Russocentrism that had haunted him during the discussion of the "National Question" were proven beyond a shadow of a doubt. In 1946, his poems and essays were published as *Collected Works*.

☙❧

THE GLOW of victory wasn't enough to quell his innate paranoia, and he worried that returning POWs might have been exposed to too many Western ideas and would pose a threat to the Soviet system. "Filtration" camps were established, and all returning soldiers were questioned there to see if they were traitors. Of the 2,775,700 men interrogated, about half were sent to labor camps.

꧁꧂

IN THE BALTIC, Stalin ordered the familiar anti-kulak and anti-religious programs he had instituted before the war. Between 1945 and 1949, nearly 142,000 people were internally exiled to Siberia. Meanwhile, he ordered the NKVD to catalog the considerable damage done to the USSR by the war. The scope of the damage was such that he found it necessary to make certain concessions to encourage loyalty among the people. He allowed the Church to continue to operate the churches they had opened during the war, and he extended the new policy of greater artistic freedom. He instituted economic reforms aimed at encouraging reconstruction, and capital punishment was abolished in 1947 (although it was reinstated in 1950).

꧁꧂

STALIN'S HEALTH began to fail, and he developed a heart condition that required him to take a two-month vacation at his dacha. He became concerned that his apparent weakness would encourage senior political and military figures to try to remove him from power. To forestall this, he prevented any of these possible enemies from gaining power or prestige, and he bugged their apartments to listen around the clock for signs of treason. The political leadership of Leningrad was accused of treason, and it was for these unfortunate individuals that the death penalty was resumed. Almost all of the accused were executed in 1950.

꧁꧂

HE SET about purging the Central Committee of suspected enemies and traitors. He demoted Molotov and appointed his trusted associates Beria and Malenkov to key positions. He brought Nikita Khrushchev to Moscow from Ukraine and made him a Central Committee secretary and head of the Moscow branch of the party.

❧

FAMINE STRUCK AGAIN IN 1946, due in part to drought and bad harvests, but also due to Stalin's policies of exporting and stockpiling food. Nearly 1.5 million people died in this iteration of hunger.

❧

THE SOVIET UNION once more began to boom, with many infrastructure projects springing up, almost all of them built with prison labor. There are no figures related to the number of deaths suffered by these virtual slaves.

❧ VIII ❧
COLD WAR

❦

When we hang the capitalists they will sell us the rope we use. Joseph Stalin

❦

The deep distrust that had bloomed between the United States and the USSR was intensified when the Soviets performed their first successful atomic bomb test in August 1949. Stalin took an intense personal interest in the development of the bomb, and his bellicose outlook was reflected in the steady growth of the Red Army. In 1949, there were 2.9 million Red Army soldiers; by 1953, there were 5.8 million.

❦

When the United Nations was formed in 1949, the Soviet Union was made a permanent member of the Security Council.

US VERSUS USSR

꧁꧂

The United States launched a program called the Marshall Plan, which was designed to undermine Soviet influence worldwide. The Soviets, meanwhile, attempted to extend their influence despite the interference of their western adversary. They attempted to woo the people in the lands they had annexed by recognizing them as independent nation-states beneath the mantle of the USSR, and by waiting to install Soviet governments by force. Stalin believed that by making the Soviet style look appealing, the Marxists in these countries would rise up to support him. Unfortunately, Marxists were thin on the ground, since most of them had been rounded up and murdered by the Nazis during occupation.

꧁꧂

DURING THIS TIME PERIOD, Stalin rarely left Moscow.

Foreign dignitaries were obligated to come to him if they wanted to meet face to face. He did not attend a September 1947 meeting of Eastern European leaders in Syklarska, Poland, that was intended to coordinate communists across Europe. The Communist Information Bureau ("Cominform") was founded at that meeting.

❧

THE MATTER of what to do with Germany remained a sticking point. Stalin hoped for a unified and demilitarized state, which ideally would fall under Soviet influence. He was unable to get the UK and the US to agree to leave Germany intact, and to try to force their hands, he set up a blockade around Berlin in June 1948. The blockade was rendered useless by the Berlin Airlift, when the US and UK sent supplies into the city via aircraft. Stalin·lifted the blockade in May 1949.

❧

IN SEPTEMBER 1949, the western powers created the Federal Republic of Germany. Not to be outdone, Stalin declared the existence of the German Democratic Republic. The UK and USA intended for Poland to be a free and independent country, and they attempted to organize an election for a new Polish government. The Soviets combined disparate workers' and socialist parties into the Polish United Workers' Party, then used vote rigging to ensure that the Communists won the election. They pursued the same policy in Hungary and Czechoslovakia, cheating the system so that the Communist parties gained control.

❧

WITH THE FORMATION of the Eastern Bloc, Churchill noted that an "Iron Curtain" had fallen across Europe. The name stuck.

FOREIGN ALLIES AND THE
KOREAN WAR

❦

The Communist Party under Mao Zedong took control of China in 1949, and in December of that year, Chairman Mao came to Moscow to meet with Stalin. By January, a new peace treaty had been signed between the two countries. They agreed to mutual support and cooperation, something that would soon be put into play.

❦

THE UNITED NATIONS refused to recognize Mao's China, and for that reason, the Soviet Union boycotted the UN.

❦

KOREA HAD BELONGED to Imperial Japan prior to the war, and after Japan surrendered, it was partitioned into north and south along the 38th parallel, each with its own government. Both claimed to be the only legitimate government of Korea, and both had heavy clients – democratic South Korea was allied with the US, and communist North Korea had the backing of China and the Soviet Union. The leader of North Korea, Kim Il-Sung, visited Stalin in Moscow in March 1949, asking for Soviet support if he invaded the south. Stalin wavered, but finally agreed in May 1950.

❧

THE NEXT MONTH, North Korea invaded South Korea. China funneled support to the North Koreans, but Stalin, more circumspect and wishing to avoid direct confrontation with the US, sent only sparse assistance. The US went to the UN, unburdened by the presence of the boycotting Soviets, and requested assistance in defending South Korea against its invaders. The UN promised troops, and an international force led by the US pushed the North Koreans back to the 38th parallel, where they had begun. Stalin convinced Mao and Kim to hold at that line, and the hostilities ceased without benefit of a treaty or peace plan. Technically, the Koreas are still at war.

❧

IN 1948, the Soviet Union was one of the first nations to recognize the new state of Israel. Premier Golda Meir came to Moscow to meet Stalin, and she was greeted by exultant crowds of Soviet Jews. The adoration his Jewish citizens showed was irksome to him, and when relations with Israel deteriorated as Israel and the United States grew closer, Stalin launched an anti-Semitic campaign in the courts and in the press. He dissolved the Jewish Anti-Fascist Committee and held a show trial for some of its members. He began to see all Jews as part of a counter-revolutionary nation with loyalties to the United States. Anti-Semitism would color all of his policies from that date forward.

⚜

AT THIS TIME, Stalin was frequently in ill health, and he took more and more long vacations at his dacha. He distrusted his doctors, most of whom were Jewish, and when one of them suggested in 1952 that he should retire to spare his health, Stalin had the man deported.

⚜

IN SEPTEMBER 1952, Stalin ordered the arrest of multiple Kremlin doctors who were accused of plotting to kill Party officials. Most of these doctors were Jewish. Stalin ordered them to be tortured to procure confessions, and the majority of the defendants were exiled.

⚜

THE SHOW TRIALS CONTINUED. In November 1952, the Slásnský Trial took place in Czechoslovakia. Thirteen senior communist party officials, eleven of them Jewish, were arrested and charged with being part of a "Zionist-American" conspiracy to destroy the Soviet Union and the Eastern Bloc. He tried Jewish workers in the Ukraine as "wreckers" and purged the Georgian Communist Party, which resulted in 11,000 deportations.

❧ IX ❧

ALL THINGS MUST END

❦

Gratitude is a sickness suffered by dogs.
Joseph Stalin

❦

Stalin was aware that his time was running short. His health
had been failing for a long while, and he was concerned with
the direction the Soviet Union would take in his absence. He
published *The Economic Problems of Socialism in the USSR* in
1952, a book meant to provide instructions for the party to
follow after his death.

❦

In October of that year, he gave one of his last speeches to the Central Committee. He described the qualities that a successor should have and denounced the men who were in line to follow him, especially Molotov and Mikoyan.

❧

One of his last acts was to eliminate the Politburo and replace it with a larger version called the Presidium.

DEATH COMES CALLING

❧❧❧

On March 1, 1953, Stalin was found on the floor of his bedroom, semi-conscious. He had suffered a massive cerebral hemorrhage that had damaged his ability to move or communicate. He was moved to a couch in his study and stayed there for three days while he was spoon fed and leeched.

❧❧❧

HIS CHILDREN SVETLANA and Vassily arrived the next day, but Vassily was drunk and was sent away. Svetlana stayed by his side. Stalin passed away on March 5, 1953.

❧❧❧

HIS DEATH WAS ANNOUNCED on March 6, 1953, and for three days his body lay in state before it was transferred to Lenin's mausoleum. There was such a press to see his body that one hundred mourners were crushed to death by crowds. China declared a day of mourning in his honor.

LEGACY

※

Stalin has been called one of the greatest monsters of the twentieth century, which is something of an accomplishment, considering that he has Adolf Hitler and Pol Pot as challengers for that title. There is no disputing that he had the blood of millions on his hands. The numbers given for his body count range from three million to fifteen million, all victims of Soviet policies that Stalin personally put into practice.

※

HE WAS A DICTATOR, RUTHLESS, "TEMPERAMENTALLY CRUEL," resentful, vindictive, paranoid, and a possible sociopath. (Several armchair psychologists have posited that he suffered from sociopathic personality traits at the least and outright insanity at the worst.) He left scars that will never heal.

❦

FOR ALL THE harm he did, he is also remembered fondly by many in Russia today for his capabilities as a nation builder. He brought the Soviet Union from backwater to world power, a feat that should earn him some admiration, however grudging. He was determined, as his record of escapes from Tsarist prisons shows, and he was charming, a talented actor and an accomplished liar. He was a great organizer and a hard worker, traits that helped him build the USSR from the ground up.

❦

WHAT IS LEFT to be said about Joseph Stalin? He was a mercurial and complex man, but he was also a wounded child. His hatred of the bourgeoisie and the Tsar, his suspicious nature and his tendency to take umbrage at the least offense can all be seen as legacies of his miserable childhood. Children who suffer the trauma of abusive parents grow up to be people who see ulterior motives and dangers in every corner, whether or not these threats actually exist. Stalin's paranoia and grudge-holding are almost hallmark traits for abused children who reach adulthood.

❦

MOST ABUSED CHILDREN who develop pathological defense mechanisms don't achieve the heights of power that Stalin reached. It may be that Stalin's cruelty wasn't the exception; the exception was his ability to visit it upon the masses.

FOR FURTHER READING...

- Barmine, Alexander (1945). *One Who Survived*. New York: G. P. Putnam.
- Bell, P.M.H. (2011). *Twelve Turning Points of the Second World War*. New Haven and London: Yale University Press.
- Conquest, Robert (1991). *Stalin: Breaker of Nations*. New York and London: Penguin Books.
- Hayward, Joel (1998). *Stopped at Stalingrad*. Kansas City: University of Kansas Press.
- Khlevniuk, Oleg V. (2015). *Stalin: New Biography of a Dictator*. Translated by Nora Seligman Favorov. New Have and London: Yale University Press.
- Kirvosheev, G. F. (1997). *Soviet Casualties and Combat Losses in the Twentieth Century*. New York: Greenhill Books.
- Kort, Michael (2010). *The Soviet Colossus*. New York: M. E. Sharpe.

- Montefiore, Simon Sebag (2003). *Stalin: The Court of the Red Tsar*. London: Weidenfeld & Nicolson.
- Montefiore, Simon Sebag (2007). *Young Stalin*. London: Weindenfeld & Nicolson.
- Orlov, Alexander (1953). *The Secret History of Stalin's Crimes*. New York: Random House.
- Roberts, Geoffrey (2006). *Stalin's Wars: From Word War to Cold War, 1939-1953*. New Haven and London: Yale University Press.
- Service, Robert (2004). *Stalin: A Biography*. London: Macmillan.

YOUR FREE EBOOK!

As a way of saying thank you for reading our book, we're offering you a free copy of the below eBook.

Happy Reading!

Made in the USA
Columbia, SC
11 July 2023

20272151R00067